Catalyst

CATALYST

Sparking Light from Darkness

Through Faith, Healing, and Story

A Self Help Memoir

Brooke

Copyright © 2025 by Brooke

All rights reserved. No part of this book may be reproduced, stored, or transmitted in any form—electronic, mechanical, photocopying, recording, or otherwise—without written permission from the author, except for brief quotes used in reviews or articles.

ISBN: 979-8-9940506-0-6

Legal Disclosure:

This book is a memoir based on the author's personal experiences, memories, and reflections. Certain names, identifying details, timelines, and events have been changed, combined, or generalized to protect the privacy of individuals and to prevent identification.

All statements in this work reflect the author's subjective perceptions, interpretations, and emotional experiences at the time and are not intended to be factual assertions about any individual's character, conduct, or intent.

Any dialogue included is a reconstruction based on memory and is not intended to represent verbatim conversations. Descriptions of events and people are presented through the author's personal perspective and should be understood as such.

This work is not intended to harm, defame, or misrepresent any person. Any resemblance to actual individuals is based solely on the author's personal experience and interpretation.

To the extent any statements may be interpreted as factual, they are made without intent to assert verifiable claims and are instead expressions of the author's perspective.

Acknowledgments:

To my dearest boy, you are such a light in my life and my greatest inspiration. I don't know what I did to deserve the brightest boy and greatest muse. It is because of you that I have healed, grown, and seen the brightest light I've ever seen radiate from a single soul.

Keep shining bright, my little star.

To my mom, Sissy, and Mamo: Thank you for your endless love and support. You have shown me what strength and resilience really are.

To all of those who have helped me along the way.

Catalyst:

Sparking Light From Darkness

Prologue: Finding My Light - Age 26

I didn't always believe my life would become something meaningful.

There was a time when everything felt uncertain—when the ground beneath me kept shifting, and I didn't know who I was becoming.

I wasn't searching for purpose. I was trying to get through each day.

What I didn't know then was this: the very things I was trying to escape would become the foundation of what I would one day build.

I looked in the mirror, and there it was—the light in my eyes again.

Just a flicker beneath the dark circles, but it was there.

The dark circles weren't from heartbreak or sleepless nights spent replaying pain; they were from the quiet thrill of creating—of writing, imagining, dreaming again. It was almost two in the morning, and my mind was alive.

What once felt like something that would consume me had quietly become something I could create from.

There were seasons when that spark disappeared completely. The light in my eyes had been drowned by tears, dimmed by worry, buried under the weight of everything I couldn't fix. This isn't a story about conquering darkness or becoming someone untouchable. It's about finding my way back to light, again and again, and realizing that darkness wasn't the enemy—it was the catalyst. What I feared most was quietly shaping me into someone stronger and more aware.

I didn't always have the words for it. There were nights I sat just like this—broken, crying, exhausted—not from creating, but from heartbreak. From endings I didn't want, from the helplessness of knowing I couldn't make someone change or stay. My therapist once told me, *"You'd rather feel guilt than helplessness."* She was right.

Guilt made me feel in control—like if I'd just done something differently, maybe things wouldn't have fallen apart. But helplessness…that meant surrender.

What I didn't know then was that surrender would become my greatest teacher.

I've learned that some of our deepest inspiration is born from the ashes of what broke us. At the time, I thought darkness meant something was wrong with my life. Looking back, it was what taught me how to recognize light in the first place.

When I was at my lowest, I remember my sister saying, "When you hit rock bottom, the only way to go is up." I rolled my eyes then—it felt hollow, like something people say because they don't know what else to say. But she was right. At rock bottom, there's nowhere left to fall. All you can do is look up, even when all you see is black.

For a long time, I could only see the walls around me—the well I'd fallen into. Now, years later, I understand that those dark walls taught me to find my way toward the light again. I've come to believe that darkness isn't the opposite of light; it's the contrast that helps us see it more clearly.

Maybe our darkest moments are just preparation—softening us, deepening us, shaping us into people who can hold compassion for others still lost in theirs. Maybe if we could see the purpose in real time, we'd resist it, control it, ruin the lesson. But life has a way of working things out—not how or when we expect, but somehow, perfectly.

My grandma—my fiery, stubborn Mamo—taught me that stories are how we make sense of it all. She wasn't your typical cookie-baking grandma. She was fierce and unfiltered, with a spine of steel and a heart that never gave up. I grew up listening to her stories, realizing that each one was a lifeline—proof that pain and resilience can coexist.

We are all living stories, intertwining with others' stories in ways we don't always understand. I don't believe in coincidences. There's something greater at work—some call it the universe; I call

Him God, the creator of the universe. The one who *is* love and light. The Lord always connects the dots, even when we can't see the full picture yet.

A sign I once saw at my friend's mom's house read:

> "Either everything is a miracle, or nothing is."

I choose to believe everything is.

That belief led me to start LifeStories Heirlooms—an heirloom creation brand that helps others preserve their stories before they're lost. Because every story matters. Every voice matters. Sometimes the simple act of telling our story is the bridge between isolation and connection—between pain and purpose.

I used to think darkness ended when the traumatic event ended or when I poured my heart out in therapy. But I've realized that the truth is as long as we are here on this earth we are going to face darkness. The funny thing is that even my journey into entrepreneurship was sparked from the darkness of an unexpected layoff right before Thanksgiving. It was difficult but my past hardships gave me the strength and the faith that, even though it was difficult to see in the moment, losing my job would catalyze me into something I always felt called to do. Now, here I am a year later with two businesses, a podcast, and now this book. Losing my job wasn't the end. It was just the beginning and sometimes we lose things to make space for bigger and better things that are coming our way.

As someone who helps others share their stories, it only feels right to share mine. Not because I'm special—but because I'm not. We all carry pain. We all face darkness. But we also all have the ability to find light again.

If even one person reads this and feels seen, then it mattered.

To live is to feel pain. To live is to love and lose, to fall and rise, to break and rebuild. It's to hold both heartbreak and laughter in the same breath. It's to find beauty in imperfection, meaning in chaos, and purpose in pain.

This is not a story of perfection—it's a story of overcoming and becoming.

A story of darkness transforming into light.

Of learning that even when the spark fades, it can always be reignited.

P.S.: After every chapter, you'll find reflection prompts. I intentionally left space for you to write directly in these pages, because healing is a conversation between your story and mine. Our lives are more connected than we realize, and it's a beautiful thing when our experiences weave together on the same page.

If your handwriting is big and messy like mine,

feel free to grab extra paper — no judgment here. My hope is that these pages become a place of honesty, hope, softness, and maybe even a few well-timed laughs.

You'll also notice that my pen name is *Brooke*. I chose it for a few reasons. Yes, every story matters — that's why I founded LifeStories Heirlooms — but I also believe we're all human beings living in a complicated, imperfect world. Every one of us is touched in some way by suffering — whether through abuse, trauma, divorce, addiction, financial hardship, or loss.

On a personal note, neither of the last names I've carried fully feel like they belong to me. Names can hold history, but they don't have to hold identity.

I chose *Brooke* as a reminder that we are not defined by the labels we're given, the families we come from, the relationships we've been in, or the chapters we've lived through.

We are defined by who we become — by the light we grow into, not the names stamped on paper.

And if you changed a few details, this story could belong to anyone.

Pain is universal... but so are smiles and the ability to rise from it.

Chapter 1: The First Spark

My story didn't begin under perfect circumstances. But then again, few beginnings ever do.

Life has a funny way of intertwining the most unexpected paths—not always to last, but sometimes to create something meant to be. Out of that meeting came me.

From the very start, life seemed to weave together both light and shadow, beauty and uncertainty. If you look at the first picture of my sister—my Sissy—and me together, she looks sad, lonely, tired. When my mom announced her pregnancy, her response was, "I don't want a baby brother or sister! I want a baby snake instead!"

My beginnings weren't polished or picture-perfect, but they were deeply human—messy, complicated, and full of heart.

When I was born, my sister wanted to name me *Butterfly.* That contrast makes me smile even now—how resistance so quickly became affection.

For an entire week after I was born—that Tuesday in April—my first and middle names were switched. I was Alexandrea Brooke. Then the hospital called to inform my mom that they had forgotten to have my father sign the birth certificate, and she excitedly said, "So it hasn't been filed with the state yet? I could change her name?!"

So that's what she did. After a week of mulling over *Alexandrea*—and realizing everyone would probably end up calling me Alex, Lexi, or Andrea—she had second thoughts. Everyone in my family is tall, so my mom pictured me growing up to be this towering woman that people might call *Big Al*. Let's just say that image alone was enough to make her change my name.

She decided I was meant to be a Brooke—a babbling one at that. It couldn't have been more fitting. My life has moved like that brook—sometimes calm, sometimes turbulent, but always forward.

My arrival wasn't easy. My mom's pregnancy was complicated and risky, but even in the midst of fear, there was love. There was hope. There was faith that something beautiful could grow from uncertainty.

Even before I understood it, my life carried this thread of transformation—a beginning that wasn't perfect, but purposeful. I believe now that some of the most beautiful stories are written in imperfect ink, the kind that bleeds, stains, and still somehow tells the truth.

Light was already forming quietly, even then.

Reflection Prompt:

What beginnings in your life have surprised you with their hidden beauty?

How has imperfection shaped your story for the better?

Chapter 2: The Day the Light Dimmed

I don't remember every detail of my early years, but I remember how they felt.

There was a shadow that settled in long before I had words for it — a kind of quiet confusion that made the world feel less safe than it should have. I learned early that not every smile meant safety, and not every person could be trusted. I didn't understand it then, but I carried that *knowing* in my body.

Anxiety became my way of creating control in times I didn't feel safe. I counted things—windows, doors, patterns — as if order could protect me with distraction. Obsessive thoughts became my way of building walls in moments where I felt my sense of safety and boundaries were shaken. Looking back, I can see it for what it was: my body trying to create safety before I knew how to.

The fear of men, the need for control, the icky feeling in the depth of my stomach that never seemed to fully leave when I was around someone who didn't feel safe to me — they all had roots in a darkness I couldn't name yet.

For years, I didn't see it for what it was. I thought these thought patterns and feelings were just normal. But deep down, I was a child trying to make sense of something that made no sense.

When I look back now, I see how much that unspoken wound shaped my early life. It made me cautious, hyper-aware, and careful with my trust. It also made me resilient. Even as fear told me the world wasn't safe, something inside me whispered—there has to be more than this.

That small voice — that spark — is what kept me alive inside.

I didn't know it then, but those anxious patterns were really my brain's way of keeping me safe. They were a map through the darkness until I could find real safety later in life.

Even before I understood it, I was learning how to live with uncertainty — how to build safety in my own mind when the world around me felt unpredictable.

The people I loved most were human too — imperfect, fragile, and sometimes lost in their own pain. I didn't know it then, but the cracks that were forming in my foundation would soon become earthquakes.

For years, I didn't understand it and tried to suppress it or explain it away with logic, but I now realize that these were the ways I learned early to listen to my body—the way my stomach tightened when something felt off, the way my chest constricted when the air around me changed. Even as a child, I could sense when a space wasn't safe, even if I couldn't explain why. That instinct became my compass long before I understood its purpose.

For now, I just kept counting. I kept smiling, even though at 5 years old I already hated my smile and would loathe looking at my school pictures because of it. I kept surviving.

Light was still there, flickering quietly, waiting for me to find it again.

What I didn't know then was that the world would soon test every bit of that fragile safety I'd built inside myself.

Reflection Prompt:

What were the first moments in your life that made the world feel unsafe?

What coping patterns did you create to protect yourself — and how have they served or limited you since?

Chapter 3: Hollowed Places

I was in fourth grade the morning everything shifted. I came downstairs, still half-asleep, to find a suitcase sitting on the couch. My dad was packing it while my mom stood nearby, her voice quiet but tense. He looked up and saw me, surprised. A moment later, he was gone.

My mom told me it wasn't my fault—that she was there for me. I believed her, but part of me still wondered if maybe I'd done something wrong. Children have a way of turning pain inward like that.

It was 2008—the middle of the recession. My mom had been a stay-at-home mom for years, suddenly faced with rebuilding from scratch.

A month later, the day after Christmas, my father called about picking up the rest of his things. We left his boxes outside the garage, but later my mom and sister decided to bring some of them back inside so nothing would get stolen. We went out for a bit, probably to grab dinner or run errands, but when we came home, the house felt strange.

The TV was gone. The front door lock had been altered in a way that made us feel unsafe. For a moment we thought someone had broken in. I remember the mix of fear and disbelief—the feeling that even our home wasn't safe anymore.

The divorce moved forward after that. I don't remember everything from that time period, just the way my stomach twisted whenever it was time for him to pick me up. The weekends I spent with him were filled with an unease I couldn't name.

It wasn't the kind of sadness you could cry out; it was quieter than that. More like an icky feeling that sat in my stomach like a pit and didn't leave.

I learned early to brace myself for goodbyes that didn't come with closure.

Looking back now, I can see how much those moments shaped me. They taught me about instability and also resilience—the kind that grows quietly in the cracks when life falls apart. Another memory I have from 4th grade was having my writing read aloud for the class by my sweet, lovely teacher Mrs. Weaver, who was praising me for my voice that came through my writing. Even then the seeds of writing were being planted and served as a way for my voice to be heard.

That was the beginning of my abandonment wound—the ache of wanting to be chosen, to be safe, to be seen.

Reflection Prompt:

What was your first experience of loss or instability?

How did it shape the way you view safety and connection today?

Chapter 4: Butterflies Without Wings

Things eventually smoothed out after my parents' divorce, and I was able to stay in the home I'd always known with the people who felt like safety. I still remember the day of the hearing that June: I spent it running through sprinklers in my neighbor's backyard. It should have felt carefree and bright, but a quiet cloud hung over everything. Even joy felt heavier back then.

My grandma moved in with us. I'd always loved her visits, but living together was a big adjustment. We already had a cat and two dogs, and she arrived with two cats and another dog—six animals under one roof. Chaos doesn't even begin to cover it. Still, there was comfort in that full house. Despite her stubborn streak and our crowded living room, we looked out for one another.

My mom was navigating a new season—stepping into work after years of being fully present at home with us. Even if it wasn't always spoken, I could sense the weight of that transition. There were quiet conversations about money, and even as a kid, I could feel that things mattered more than they had before.

Looking back, I can see how much my mom was carrying during that time. What I experienced as her holding things together, she was navigating as responsibility—doing everything she could to provide consistency and care for our family.

There was a quiet strength in how she showed up for us, even in a season of change—something I understand far more now than I did then.

Remember in Chapter 2 when I talked about hating my kindergarten school pictures because I was insecure about my smile? That carried right into middle school. I had a genetic growth deficiency in my jaws that affected how I smiled, ate, and even spoke. It made me self-conscious. My sister—always the encourager—suggested I join theater, so I did.

Drama class became a space where I could shine. I loved performing, making people laugh, and watching a room light up. Storytelling had always been in my bones—it gave me a way to connect, to turn emotion into expression. My goofy nature finally had a stage. But when auditions came around, I was usually cast in the background. I told myself it was because of my lisp and my smile. My dream of becoming an actress began to feel out of reach.

Still, outside that classroom, the loneliness lingered.

Around the same time, I started comparing myself to the images I saw everywhere—perfect faces, flawless bodies. At five-foot-six and 145 pounds, I thought I was huge. I tried "water fasting," convinced it would make me more worthy. Looking back, I can see how young that thinking was, but at the time, it felt like the only way I could fit in and feel secure in myself.

Middle school has a way of magnifying every insecurity—especially the ones you don't yet have words for. Everyone is trying to figure out who they are while pretending they already know. I often felt invisible, too much and not enough at the same time.

Those years taught me how insecurity creeps in quietly—through money worries, comparison, silence, and fear. But they also taught me awareness. Even in the chaos, there were glimmers of connection: laughter with my sister, our pets curled at our feet, my grandma's unwavering presence. Tiny sparks that reminded me light could exist even here.

Feeling Different

Even before middle school, I'd always felt a little out of place. I was loud, goofy, and full of imagination, but I never seemed to fit into the boxes other kids lived in. My body, my smile, even my thoughts all felt slightly offbeat - "weird" as the other kids liked to call me.

April 27, 2011:

"In the movies Mackenzie told me to move so I did. In the movie I sat with no friends. There were people around but I was alone and lonely."

That memory still stings. Mackenzie was the girl everyone loved—the new girl who seemed to knock me right off my pedestal the moment she arrived in fifth grade. I still remember the day she was the only one who could answer the teacher's question "What is a philanthropist?" From then on, she was the smartest, the favorite, the one who never got in trouble and always seemed effortlessly perfect.

So when she told me to move, I did. I didn't question it. By then, I'd already learned what it meant to make myself small to stay safe—even when it hurt.

I didn't realize then that this pattern — obeying, pleasing, shrinking — was my nervous system still doing what it had learned in early childhood: that peace came from compliance.

November 30, 2011:

"I sat by myself and read and ate candy. It was a free day in that class. No one likes me."

That sentence felt true at the time. Looking back, it wasn't that I was unlikeable - it was that I hadn't found people who knew how to see me yet.

Middle school can be a cruel mirror. I was learning who I was, but I was also learning what parts of myself the world didn't always accept. My insecurities about my jaw and smile, the body image battles, the obsession with perfection — they all tied back to wanting to be seen and chosen.

The Search for Validation

When I didn't feel seen, I sought validation wherever I could find it.

August 29, 2011:

"My dreams: I wanna have an old-fashioned wedding. I want the hottest husband ever! Four kids, my first a boy."

Those early dreams make me smile now — they were innocent, but underneath was a longing for stability, for someone who wouldn't leave, and an image of the "perfect" life. My love for old-fashioned things began around this time and it's amusing that it stuck around.

Then came the crushes:

November 27, 2011:

"It's one of those relationships that you know you shouldn't like him but you do. He sucks you in with his words... I think, maybe he changed. Then I end up hurt and I think, 'stupid girl! Brooke, don't get sucked in again.'"

Even at thirteen, I recognized the cycle — hope, disappointment, self-blame. It was the same emotional rhythm I'd learned years before: confusion followed by guilt, comfort followed by fear.

At thirteen, I wrote:

"I didn't think he was that cute but then I got to know him better. He's kinda crazy, my type of guy lol!"

I can smile at that now - but even then, I was already drawn to intensity over safety. I didn't know the difference yet.

November 29, 2011:

"Things I wanna do in my life: go skydiving, kiss lots of guys, get married, have kids, be famous, write at least one book."

Those words make me laugh now — that mix of innocence, boldness, and unhealed pain. Beneath it all was the same little girl still trying to prove she was lovable.

The Worry That Never Slept

May 9, 2012:

"I always worry. And have bothers. Half the time I

don't know why. It's like I need something to worry about so I just bring up something to worry about."

That entry breaks my heart — not because it's dramatic, but because it's so familiar. My mind had been trained to expect danger, to stay alert. Worry became my way of staying safe, my brain's constant whisper that maybe if I could anticipate what might go wrong, I could prevent it.

I didn't know it then, but that was trauma, not personality.

Middle school wasn't just about crushes and cliques. It was the beginning of understanding how early pain shapes patterns — how abandonment becomes anxiety, and fear turns into control. But it was also the beginning of something else: awareness. I was learning to name what I felt. I was starting to see that the things that made me different might also be the things that made me special.

Reflection Prompts

When have I felt anxious or insecure?

What is my relationship with money and safety?

When was the first time I felt different from those around me?

How have I sought validation or safety in ways that trace back to old wounds?

What parts of my younger self still want to be seen and understood?

Chapter 5: Falling into the Fire

Although my parents' divorce hearing concluded and the ink on the final custody agreement dried years before, my world began to shift again when a new person entered the picture.

My father met someone new and from where I sat as a teenager, the legal landscape of my life seemed to change quickly. Custody arrangements I had grown used to were being challenged. As someone who has always believed in listening to the voice of children, my mom advocated for a child family investigator so that I could have my opinion heard on the matter as a high schooler. But what unfolded next felt, to me, like my own words were being used in ways I hadn't expected.

The courts became a heavy weight in the background of my life during a time that should have been filled with ordinary teenage memories.

I want to be clear: I'm sharing how this felt to live through, not making claims about anyone's motives or intentions. I only know what it was to be the child standing in the middle of it.

December 16, 2014 – The Worst Day

Finals week. Sophomore year.

My sister and I had plans to go Christmas shopping after school. She pulled up to my high school in her red Audi; the air inside smelled like sweet Hawaiian vanilla.

A knot formed in my stomach. What should have been a light, sisterly drive filled with talk of gifts and holidays was heavy with something else. I felt the heaviness between us before my sister even spoke the words,

> "We have to go home," she said quietly. "You have two hours to pack. The judge ordered that you move in with your dad and his fiancée."

Contact with my family was suddenly restricted in ways that felt extreme to me.

There were forces at play I didn't understand — decisions made in rooms I wasn't old enough to sit in, but that shaped my entire world.

I remember tears more than words.

I walked into the only home I'd ever known—Mom and Mamo at the kitchen table, both crying.

Overwhelm. Disbelief. Shock.

I must have packed, but I couldn't tell you what. It's as if that version of me dissolved in those two hours.

When the Body Remembers

Even now, healed as I am, my body still tells the story my mind would rather forget.

A sinking feeling in my belly.

Racing in my chest.

Words being choked by tightness closing in around my throat.

The pounding in the right side of my head that has followed me for years.

The body remembers what words can't.

Images flicker — moments that felt physically and emotionally overwhelming to me—intense, unpredictable, and frightening in ways I didn't fully understand at the time. I no longer need to describe each scene to know what they meant: fear, powerlessness, violation, confusion.

The Goodbye

Stepping outside that evening felt like stepping off a cliff.

The three people who had always loved me most walked me to the truck waiting in the driveway. My sister hugged me tight and whispered, *"Give them hell for me."*

She reminded me that Anne Frank wrote through her captivity — that words could be a window even when walls closed in.

Then I let go of the hug, and of everything familiar.

The Ride

I climbed into the truck, the knot in my stomach tightening until it felt like rope around my throat. I remember being asked to hand over my phone, and I did — fear first, courage later.

A few miles down the highway in rush-hour traffic, I reached for the phone, desperate for connection to my familiar life and some sense of control. What followed was tense and frightening for me. I remember loud words, the feeling of the situation escalating, and a quiet that felt louder than any shouting.

We drove on through rush-hour traffic and the loudest quiet I've ever known.

Aftermath

At the house that wasn't home, I locked myself in a bedroom and cried until there were no tears left.

My head throbbed so hard I thought it might split.

Before dawn, I was woken for finals. The drive to school blurred with the sound of *Iris* by the Goo Goo Dolls — Mom's favorite song.

Later that week, I sat in "reintegration therapy," trying to explain how much it hurt to be taken from everything I loved.
I told him I cried on the way to school.

His only response:

> "I saw you get a little misty-eyed earlier."

In that environment, I started to believe my feelings didn't matter. So I adapted the only way I knew how - I became quiet.

The days that followed felt like living inside a nightmare I couldn't wake up from.

Reality Set In

The courtroom had become a stage where narratives were crafted by people who didn't know my heart. Terms I didn't fully understand at the time were introduced into the proceedings, and they seemed to carry significant weight in decisions being made about my life.

I remember feeling like my voice didn't matter to anyone but my mom. I knew where I felt safe. I knew where I was happiest. But those truths didn't seem to weigh as much as everything else happening around me.

Factors in the legal process that felt beyond my control"

Life in that environment felt tense, unpredictable, and emotionally hard for me. None of that was visible from the outside. On paper, everything looked polished and proper. What I didn't understand at the time was how little control I actually had — and how decisions could be made about my life without anyone fully understanding what it felt like to live inside it.

Behind closed doors, my experience was very different from how things may have looked from the outside.

I don't write this to blame or accuse — but because it is the truth of the child I was. A child who learned far too early that systems don't always protect the people who need it most.

Reintegration

The room was bright, sterile, too quiet. We sat in chairs arranged to suggest cooperation but built for confusion. I was told, in so many words, that background equals gratitude and that money spent on me should buy compliance. I stared at my hands and practiced the only safety I knew—silence. A silence that felt like the same pit in my stomach that grew branches into my throat to stifle my words to keep me safe. Just like I learned in my early childhood at the age of 3.

I sat there wondering if love had a price tag.

Each morning, I woke up in a house that wasn't home. My stomach ached constantly — part anxiety, part grief. The walls felt tight, the silence heavy. I started to believe I was a burden, that maybe I wasn't meant to be alive at all. Through tears, I'd give in to the dark thoughts that all of this was my fault and my family would be better off without me. I began to view myself as the root of their suffering and wanted it all to end.

In the white sterile room, the silence was broken by the "therapist's" voice.

"So, I hear you're suicidal", he blurted out as he stared me down.

"Yes." I responded.

"Well, how would you do it? Because if you're gonna do it you'd want to do it right. Otherwise, you'll end up in the hospital with a bunch of crazies."

Not even the "family therapist" was safe.

I'd look in the mirror and barely recognize the girl staring back. Tears would fall, and I'd whisper, How could anyone ever love me?

Now I know the answer was there all along: Jesus loves us, even when we're too broken to love ourselves. He doesn't turn away from our pain — He sits with us in it, crying with us, waiting for the day we see ourselves through His eyes again.

Fragments of the Fire

December 17, 2014:

"They took my phone to put 'parental controls' on it. She said it's either that or a flip phone.

This isn't my home and it never will be.

I remember interpreting certain conversations in a way that made me feel like I had to comply or risk consequences. Whether or not that was the intention, it created a deep sense of fear and instability in me.

I hide all my feelings and act happy just to make them happy, even though

I'm really sad below the surface.

I have to hide it and be fake, just like them."

December 18, 2014:

"I'm not allowed to go to my Spirit Squad Christmas party or perform at the Nuggets game unless my attitude improves.

They said I could be hospitalized for being a threat to myself and others.

But anybody is dangerous if you fuel the sparks in their soul."

Those journal entries were my only form of proof, my only control in a house that monitored everything I said or did.

There were moments where interactions escalated in ways that felt physically and emotionally overwhelming to me. I remember feeling powerless in my own body—like I had no control over what was happening or how to respond.

And still, I survived.

Somehow, I always knew to protect my journal.
That voice inside me — that guardian angel — kept me safe more than once.
I often felt like my privacy wasn't fully my own.

A Star in the Night

It was about a week after I'd been taken away. The house was heavy with silence — the kind that hums with unspoken rules.

I was told I didn't deserve to go to church.
Something about that word — *deserve* — cut deeper than the rest.

So, I left.

It was Christmas Eve, and the night air burned cold against my skin.
I walked nearly two miles alone, through streets lit by holiday lights that didn't feel meant for me.
I wore leggings and a T-shirt, my breath sharp in the dark, my skin blotched with anxiety rashes.
I didn't know what I was looking for — only that I needed to find it.

When I finally reached the church, everyone else was dressed up, glowing in candlelight and sequins, surrounded by families.

I slipped quietly into the back pew, small and trembling.

Then the music began.

We three kings of Orient are, bearing gifts we traverse afar...

The words floated through the sanctuary like a message meant just for me.

Star of wonder, star of night, star with royal beauty bright.

Goosebumps rippled down my arms as tears filled my eyes.

In that moment, I felt something I hadn't felt since before everything fell apart — presence. Not safety, not certainty, but the quiet comfort of light in the darkness.

The light was still there.

Maybe faint, but alive.

And even if I couldn't see where it would lead yet,

I knew faith had found me again — walking alone,

under a star bright enough to break the dark.

My father and his fiancée thought material things could buy peace. Clothes, shoes, gifts — little distractions wrapped in ribbons. For a moment, they made me feel seen. But as soon as the newness faded, I was emptier than before.

That's the thing about pain — you can't cover it with things. You have to face it.

Fragments from My Younger Self

2014

"When you look at her, what do you see?

When you hear her laugh, what do you hear?

You probably think she's just a happy, bubbly girl who doesn't care what anyone thinks.

But you're wrong.

Behind these blue-gray eyes, there's a storm—thoughts, worries, confusion.

She knows everybody, yet feels lonely.

She used to care too much, but after too many avalanches, her heart froze.

She laughs herself to tears, then cries herself to sleep.

No one knows my battles.

Maybe I don't even know myself."

Reading those words now feels like looking into the eyes of a ghost—a younger version of me still trying to make sense of a world that didn't feel fair or safe.

But inside all that pain, I can also see resilience. I can see the beginnings of the woman I was becoming—curious, observant, endlessly introspective.

A Spark in the Dark

During this darkest time of my life my sister left me a note, *"I promise everything will be OK you're such a smart intelligent young lady full of potential. You have the spark inside of you to make someone* *laugh even on their worst day. You're a very special girl and the future has so many good and exciting things in store for you. Just hang on every now and again life isn't going to be perfect you're not being punished, it's more like a test and I know you'll pass because you're very strong we all have moments in life where we are tested I love you don't ever lose your **spark**. Everything will be great and God will always be there for you."*

One night, as I spiraled into an abyss of self blame and felt completely alone and purposeless, I asked God to give me a dream.

"Show me what I'm meant for," I whispered through tears.

That night, I dreamt I was back in my high school math classroom.

***

From somewhere above, I could see myself —

a quiet, sad girl, sitting at her desk.

Then a man's voice asked gently,

'Brooke, what is your calling in life?'

I saw myself smile faintly, turn my head, look into

my own eyes, and say,

'My calling in life is to help people.'

***

I woke up with peace in my chest — a peace that whispered, *you are still meant for something.*

Reflection

That night carved something deep inside me.

It taught me that sometimes survival means walking straight through fire you never asked for.

It also taught me the power of witnessing my own story — because even when no one else sees your pain, naming it is the first spark of healing.

Reflection Prompts

When has my body remembered what my mind wanted to forget?

What moment forced me to grow before I was ready?

How can I turn my pain into something that witnesses others?

Chapter 6: Light in the Ward

Three months passed and I was still in the pit of fire with no way out. Reintegration therapy, manipulation, emptiness, anxiety mixed with severe depression. A perfect recipe for despair. That March afternoon I visited my school resource officer to just have someone to talk to.

"I don't want to live anymore."

As those words fell out of my mouth, my confidant looked at me from across the table, paused, and explained that he would have to put me on a 72 hour mental health hold.
My world was already so confusing and then to have to leave school abruptly in a police car added

even more chaos to the mix. But hey, I was already in the darkest time of my life so how much worse could it get?

I said goodbye to, who I thought was, my best friend and begged her not to tell anyone where I was going. I stepped out of the school and into a cop car and the unknown. It was scary yet a relief that I was going somewhere outside the house of darkness.

When the Body Speaks

Inside the hospital, the doors locked behind me—and, strangely, I felt safer. Structure can be a kind of mercy. So can strangers who listen.

"For once, the locked doors felt like protection, not punishment."

There were group sessions and strict routines, but also laughter. We sang in the showers. My signature song was "Tomorrow" from Annie the musical. We traded tea tags like tiny fortunes, each quote a permission slip to hope. One boy reminded me of my cousin and made me feel less alone. Another made us laugh so hard that I hit my fist against my tray and spilled juice across the table. People saw me as I was—a teenager with a storm inside, not a problem to be fixed.

*"I actually feel happier than I have in a long time… like I'm understood." **(March 3, 2015)***

In the quiet hours, I wrote lists—reasons to live, lessons to keep, dreams I refused to surrender.

Perseverance

Break me down but still I rise

Like an angel I'll fly so high

Pick on me when I am weak

But trust my word I am never meek

Don't give notice to my need

But no matter what I'll still proceed

On my journey through this life

I'll never pick up a knife

Give me every reason to be filled with hate

But I let all of my feelings disintegrate

Until I am left almost completely numb

You may say that I am dumb

For still having hope—

But that is how I cope.

How I put a smile on my face

When nothing in my life feels safe.

I'm still nice to everyone,

Even though all I want is to be done.

My life is spiraling out of control,

But I'll never allow myself to be put on parole.

No matter how many times I wanted to die

Or how many times a day I cry,

I'm still here. Although I often fear what my future holds,

I'll never be shaped into one of their molds.

Never give up the fight—

Because there's always a light

At the end of the tunnel,

No matter how narrow the funnel.

Now pull yourself together,

You're not a dainty feather.

I can make it through this,

And life will be pure bliss.

(February 15, 2015)

I wrote to my future self as if I could mail her a lifeline:

"If you're reading this, you made it. Be the mom you dreamed of. Write the book. Love yourself. Keep your spark." (Spring 2015)

The hospital wasn't a fairytale. It was fluorescent and noisy and imperfect. But it gave me language. It gave me witnesses. It gave me a fragile kind of freedom.

Friends in the Ward

I met kids who had lived a thousand lifetimes in fifteen years. We swapped stories, advice, and inside jokes. We learned that kindness is a currency that never runs out.

When I cried, girls stepped out of their rooms—against the rules—and wrapped me in the simple miracle of presence.

"People here are strong. Some have been through more than I can imagine. I don't feel crazy—I feel human." (March 4–6, 2015)

I met people who had experienced more than I could comprehend—and yet, they were still kind.

That was my first real understanding that pain and strength can exist in the same person.

A staff member told me I was "one smart cookie." Another reminded me that structure can help a mind breathe. I wasn't broken beyond repair. I was a person whose nervous system had been on high alert for too long. That reframe mattered. It still does.

Back to the Other Side of the Fence

After about two weeks, it came time to walk through those doors and say goodbye to the place that served as a solace in the chaos with the friends who understood. It was time to go back into the darkness but it was the light from inside the ward that gave me the courage to go back to battle.

When I returned to school, I discovered that a trusted friend, the one friend I believed I could trust—the only thread to a life that still felt like mine, shared where I was after I'd asked her not to, my chest tightened. When that trust broke, it stung, another reminder that not everyone knows how to hold another person's pain. Betrayal can be unintentional and still draw blood. I learned to hold two truths at once: people are imperfect, and I can still choose to be kind and boundaried.

In therapy, I tried to explain the whiplash—how some days I felt almost normal, and other days I felt like a ghost in my own life. I shared that certain comments in reintegration sessions made me feel small, like care had conditions I could never meet. I learned to say instead: *That didn't feel safe for me.* It was a simple sentence, but it rebuilt a spine.

A Different Kind of Courage

The hospital didn't erase my pain. It taught me how to walk beside it and that I wasn't the only one carrying the invisible pain.

I learned to trust the alarms in my body and to advocate for myself with clear, gentle words.

I learned that asking for help is brave.

"I don't regret how this is playing out. I feel happier than I've felt in a long time. I'm learning a lot.

Maybe this will make me a better mom one day. A better human." (March 3–5, 2015)

Even after discharge, life stayed complicated. Some days I told myself, *maybe it's getting better.* Other days, the familiar heaviness returned. Survival sometimes looked like pretending. Something had shifted—it had been named, seen, and was beginning to return in small moments of joy. And it continued to manifest in little sparks of joy, like forming a relationship with my local Rotary club that opened me up to serving others.

I kept collecting tea tags. I kept laughing at the memory of kids who called me "valley girl" and defended me when jokes cut too deep. I kept the lists I wrote on hospital paper: reasons, gratitudes, truths. My little spark was back and I discovered an outlet for my passion of helping others.

Looking back now, I can see how those experiences shaped the way I understand people—how they think, how they react under pressure, and how behavior is often driven by unprocessed emotion rather than logic. That understanding would later become foundational in how I build, communicate, and connect in both life and business.

Reflection Prompts

Who offered me unexpected light during a dark season?

Where am I still living in *if only*—and how could I rewrite it as *even though*?

What tiny rituals (lists, songs, notes, tea tags) help me keep my spark alive?

Author's Note

This chapter reflects my memories and emotions from that time.

Some identifying details and sequences have been changed to protect privacy.

My focus is on my lived experience and the impact it had on me.

Chapter 7: Letting Go, Letting God

Someone who once broke me said, *"The two saddest words in the dictionary are if only."*

For a long time, I lived inside those words. This was the chapter where I began learning how to trade *if only* for *even though*.

If Only » Even Though

For a long time, I replayed the same loop:

If only the court had decided differently.

If only someone had listened sooner.

If only I were stronger, quieter, better.

But light doesn't bloom in *if only*. It grows in *even though*.

Even though it happened, I can heal.

Even though it hurt, I can help others.

Even though I fell into the fire, God sparked light there.

The ward gave me structure.

The kids gave me laughter.

The lists gave me language.

The tea tags gave me small, sacred rituals of hope.

And the girl I was—the one who kept writing—proved that my spark never went out. It was simply learning to breathe.

The moment I stopped trying to force the outcome — when I prayed and surrendered — was when the shift began.

The intuition (or as I like to call it, whispers from God), the faith, the writing — they were all small miracles, showing me that the power to heal was already within me because God was with me.

God wasn't asking me to be perfect.

He was asking me to *trust*. This traumatic season began to shift when I finally released my grip on control.

For so long, I had tried to force outcomes — believing that if I could just fix everything, I could finally be happy again.

But control had only destroyed my peace.

When I let go, something softened. I sparked light by accepting what I couldn't change and focusing on what I could.

Instead of being consumed by missing my family or resenting the walls around me, I poured my energy into the small joys still available to me: my high school business club, cheerleading, piano music, tea, and the quiet things that reminded me I was still me.

I stopped waiting for freedom to come from someone else. I began creating it from within.

Things were going better—until the mask slipped again.

It triggered the familiar darkness: the hopelessness, the ache that whispered, *I can't do this anymore.*

I went up to my room, tears catching in my throat.

But this time, instead of scheming or grasping for control, I picked up my pen. Instead of pointing the finger, I wrote from my heart. I poured truth onto paper, sealed it, stamped it, and let it go.

That letter to the judge wasn't an act of control. It was an act of calling.
It was the moment I put down my sword and picked up my pen — my true weapon.

After that, something inside me settled. I carried on, at peace with knowing I had stood up for myself not through blame, but through truth.

There comes a point when the fight to control everything becomes heavier than the pain itself. When you've already walked through the fire, nothing else can burn you the same way.

After so much turmoil, I stopped trying to rewrite the story. I stopped pleading for outcomes and started whispering prayers instead. Every night before bed, I prayed for peace, for protection, and for things to unfold the way they were meant to—not in the way I thought they should.

I went to school like any other teenager. I laughed with classmates, did my homework, tried to act like life was normal again. It wasn't, but I was learning to make peace with the in-between—the space between what had been and what might someday be.

And then,

I

let

Go.

I just lived my life as normally as I could given the situation. And just when I stopped trying to control everything— life reminded me I never could.

Then... I got into a car accident. It wasn't serious, but it shook me to my core because I dreaded the punishment that was coming my way.

"You need to find a way to pay for the damage."

But what it really meant was, "We have you backed into a corner. Quit your extracurriculars that are keeping you tied to an area near your mom and get a job near our house so we can show the courts that you're adapting well and need to transfer schools."

They asked what plan I came up with. I sat at the dining room table, petrified with the knot in my stomach still, but surrendering. "I don't have a plan." Heaviness filled the room.

It felt like everything was falling apart again—but this time, I wasn't the same person standing in it.

I didn't know what came next but instead of spiraling into an endless loop of doom, I distracted myself with homework and went to sleep.

The next morning there was a knock on my bedroom door. "Pack your things. You're going to stay with your grandparents. Pack as much as you can fit into your suitcase."

After being told I was "not welcome" in the house I'd been staying in for the last 11 months, I was in another house that didn't feel like home. The days blurred together. Three weeks passed quietly—filled with a strange mix of numbness, waiting, and trying to adjust to yet another version of life I hadn't chosen.

Three weeks passed and Thanksgiving was being hosted at my father's house where I wasn't welcome. My father decided that I could spend Thanksgiving with my mom since his wife didn't want me at their holiday.

Thanksgiving came and went and I was back at my grandparents' house. I prayed on my knees to Jesus and to his faithful servant Saint Jude (Judas Thaddeus, not Judas Iscariot of course). If you haven't heard of Saint Jude before, he is the patron saint of hopeless and impossible causes. He is depicted with a flame above his head representing the fervor of his love for God and the presence of the Holy Spirit within him.

In those moments on the floor of the guest room, I wasn't just praying—I was placing my situation into the hands of the saint who intercedes for what feels impossible. Or rather, what *is* impossible for humans without God.

I didn't know when anything would change.

Nothing around me shifted overnight.

But something inside me had.

For the first time, I wasn't trying to force the outcome—I was trusting that it would unfold in God's timing.

Since my father allowed me to spend Thanksgiving with my mom I asked if I could spend the weekend at her house.

December 4th. My father drove me to school that day. The air in the car was heavy and my stomach was tight. Finally he broke the silence with, "the weekend with your mom won't be happening" sliced with a sharp tone. I nodded, disappointed but not destroyed. I'd been to the darkest places already, and I knew that no matter what happened, I could survive it. There was strength in that quiet acceptance—a calm that came from surrender, not defeat.

After school, my grandmother on my father's side picked me up. I laid on her couch with a pounding headache, emotionally drained and trying to make sense of everything that had happened.

The house was quiet. Too quiet.

I remember staring at the ceiling, wondering how much longer I could keep living in this in-between.

That's when my phone rang.

It was him.

"Pack your bags," he said. "You're going with your mom. You're going back to live with her. Everything will return to the original schedule—every other weekend, if that's what you want."

In that moment, I knew—this wasn't something I had made happen. This was God.

For a second, I couldn't breathe. I just sat there, stunned. The same judge who had once ordered my removal had now signed off on my return. The same system that took me away had handed me back.

Once again I had to pack everything up in nearly an instant. Even as I prepared to leave, it didn't feel real.

My phone was unlocked. I called my mom. The words tumbled out through tears and laughter: *"I'm coming home."*

That night, I felt like a bird that had lived too long in a cage suddenly realizing the door was open. Freedom didn't come in a grand moment—it came in a simple phone call, a quiet release, a second chance. I went home and surprised my sister and enjoyed pizza with those I cherished the most.

Never underestimate the power of prayer—or the irony of a system built on human control being undone by divine timing.

Reflection Prompts

What are things that I cling to and try to control?

Why?

What would it take for me to let go of control,

even just a little bit?

What need is the sense of control filling? (It makes me feel like I'm doing something, it makes me feel less powerless, I feel less scared when I feel I can control everything, etc.)

How is my attempt to control negatively impacting my life?

Can I trust that whatever happens after letting go is meant to be and will be better than what I ever hoped for?

What would surrender *feel* like?

Chapter 8: Shedding Shadows, Growing Wings

Everyone we cross paths with leaves an imprint on us. I believe it's all part of a plan meant to shape us — even the painful parts.

Some people offer kindness that softens us. Others, even those who wound us, leave behind lessons we carry forward.

Facing the darkness means acknowledging the pain they caused and validating the feelings that came with it.

But sparking light in the darkness begins with looking for even the smallest good — not to excuse them, but to free ourselves.

For months after returning home, I didn't see him. The distance was healing. It gave me room to breathe, to find my rhythm again, to remember who I was before fear tried to define me.

But one day, that truck—the same one that had once carried me away—pulled back into view. I climbed in, heart steady but cautious. We drove in silence until he demanded my phone.

"I'm taking it for myself," he said flatly. I was left feeling like I had to figure things out on my own.

And just like that, the circle closed.

The final break wasn't loud or explosive. It was quiet—an ending that carried its own strange peace.

I was seventeen, old enough to understand that I couldn't change him, and wise enough to stop trying. There was grief, yes. The kind that sits in your chest and whispers, *you deserved more.* But there was also acceptance. The kind that says, *you have enough now.*

I needed braces and orthognathic surgery to correct my jaw so I could eat and speak without pain. I experienced significant obstacles in getting consent for the treatment I needed. It was the final refusal in a long line of them.

But this time, I didn't break.
I found my way through the system, got my treatment, and finally smiled without pain for the first time in my life.

Now when I look in the mirror, I see more than straight teeth or a healed jaw—I see proof that faith moves mountains, that peace comes after surrender, and that sometimes the very thing we try hardest to control is the thing standing in the way of our freedom.

I lost a father. But I gained myself.

And that trade, as heartbreaking as it was, became one of the most sacred exchanges of my life.

The Joy That Comes

In the middle of the storm, I found a verse that became my anchor—Romans 8:18:

"The pain that you've been feeling can't compare to the joy that is coming."

At first, I didn't fully believe it.
But with time, I began to see it unfolding in quiet ways—the soft laughter that returned, the peace that settled in my chest, the smile that no longer hurt.

That verse wasn't a promise of perfection. It was a reminder of perspective—of faith in what we cannot yet see.

Because when we finally stop gripping the steering wheel, God takes the lead.

And more often than not, He drives us somewhere better than we ever imagined.

Reflection Prompts

When have I experienced peace after surrendering control?

What "joy that is coming" might my current pain be preparing me for?

How can I begin to trust the process a little more today?

Chapter 9: Light Born from the Ashes

When I finally came home, I thought everything would instantly feel better.

But trauma doesn't end when the court orders do. It lingers — in silence, in the pauses between laughter, in the parts of you that forget how to feel safe again.

I was free, but I wasn't whole.

For a long time, I moved through life numb — smiling when expected, staying busy, mistaking distraction for healing. Anger was easier to access than pain. I told myself I was strong, but really, I was just guarded.

At eighteen, I met a boy at a concert.

The music was loud, and so was the emptiness inside me. We both came from broken places, both craving connection that felt like safety but wasn't.

What I didn't understand at the time was the difference between intensity and safety. I confused emotional highs and lows for connection, when in reality, my nervous system was responding to what felt familiar—not what was healthy.

In the beginning, I thought love could heal us both.

But love that begins in fear often turns into survival.

Our relationship became a storm — unpredictable, heavy, and full of moments that left bruises you couldn't see.

I learned to make myself small again, to avoid the next eruption.

There were days I prayed for peace and nights I clung to faith like a lifeline.

Through it all, I still believed in light — even if I couldn't always see it.

Baby Mine

Then, life gave me a reason to keep walking toward that light.

A heartbeat.

A flicker.

When I found out I was pregnant, fear and awe coexisted in my body.
But deep down, I knew — this child would be different. He felt like a promise.

The day I found out I was pregnant, it was 100 degrees and the sky was burnt orange from wildfires that couldn't be contained, just like the fear inside of me. That next morning it was snowing. In hindsight I see that this was a wink from up above that this baby would change up my world in just the way I needed, just as we needed that cold snow to bring the fires to an end. Though at the time I just felt this peace of the changing weather that only continued to soften my fear as I looked across the sidewalk and saw an all white dove who didn't fly away even when I approached with my dog.

From the moment his body and soul became one, I could sense his wild, beautiful spirit. Even in the chaos, he kicked like he already knew how to fight for the light.

I whispered to him before he was born, *"Keep shining bright, my little star."*

That Friday morning, he came into the world and changed mine forever.

The very first words spoken after his arrival were, "Well, we know his lungs work!" — and I laughed, realizing he already had his mama's loud mouth.

The doctor placed my baby boy on my chest, and in those first seconds, he lifted his tiny head, wrapped his hand around my finger, peed on me, and smiled.

There he was — my boy.

The one I had always dreamed of.

The one who made the chaos make sense.

He was — and still is — my living light.

Not because he saved me, but because he reminded me of what was worth saving.

Through his eyes, I began to see the light in myself again.

Motherhood didn't erase my pain.

It transformed it into purpose.

I began to see the world differently — softer, yet stronger.

I became fiercely protective of the light, even when it meant leaving someone else in the dark. Walking away wasn't easy.

But it was necessary.

"I want someone who brings out the best in me and fuels my spark instead of dampening it." - Brooke

September 4th, 2021

I learned that sometimes love means letting go — not out of anger, but out of clarity. I always wanted him to find the sparks of light from the ashes of his childhood wounds but for some reason I could never get him to join me on the light side.

Now, when I look at my son, I see proof that beauty can be born from brokenness.

He is living light — the joy that followed years of pain, the promise that God was still writing my story even when I thought it was over.

The pain I once tried to numb became the soil where something sacred grew.
And this time, instead of fighting for control, I chose to have faith.

A Full-Circle Healing

When my son was three, his teacher pinched him, shamed him, and told him, "Don't tell mommy or she'll think you're bad."
What matters is that when he told me, I believed him.
Without hesitation.
Without doubt.

Because once upon a time, I was three and was hurt by someone I should have been able to trust and feel safe with. My pain had prepared me to protect my son.

I took action. I stood firm. And though my heart broke all over again, it was different this time — because the little girl inside me saw what safety looked like and found her voice.

That moment, as painful as it was, became a corrective emotional experience — a sacred rewriting of my story.

The darkness I had once endured became the very thing that equipped me to bring light to my son's.

Through him, I healed pieces of myself I didn't know were still fractured.

Through him, I learned that faith is not about avoiding pain — it's about trusting that even pain can have a purpose.

Romans 8:18 says, *"The pain that you've been feeling can't compare to the joy that is coming."*

I carried that verse like a heartbeat through every storm.

And now, as I watch my son laugh, I know it was true.

The joy came.

Reflection Prompts

Where have I mistaken intensity for love?

What parts of my pain later became my purpose?

How have I been prepared by what once tried to break me?

What lessons have I learned from my children — or my inner child?

How can I trust that even what hurt me is leading me toward healing?

Who am I attracted to? What is it about them that I find attractive? Do they actually feel safe? Or just familiar?

Chapter 10: Letting Go, With Love

Before I could fully hold joy, I had to let go of people, habits, mindsets, and patterns that kept me in familiar, yet unsafe and unhealthy dynamics. In order to fully let go we cannot just ignore the feelings and suppress the past. Doing so is actually giving it more power over you and creates a recipe that looks something like this:

Recipe for a Pressure-Cooker Meltdown (Serves: One Tired Human)

Ingredients:

- 1 heaping cup of unprocessed feelings
- Several scoops of childhood wounds
- A dash of denial
- A generous pour of "I'm fine, really!"

- A sealed-tight nervous system
- Optional garnish: toxic positivity

Instructions:

1. Start by refusing to feel anything. *At all.* Pretend your emotions are like expired leftovers — if you ignore them long enough, they disappear. (Spoiler: they don't.)

2. Add a confident layer of "No seriously, I'm FINE."
Say it with enthusiasm. Add jazz hands if needed.

3. Dump all unhealed wounds into the pressure cooker.
Yes, all of them. The big ones, the small ones, the ones you swore didn't bother you anymore.

4. Seal the lid tightly.

Tighter. Even tighter. Good. Now nothing can escape — especially not common sense.

5. Turn the heat up by ignoring every squeal and whistle.

That's just your nervous system begging for attention. Totally normal. Carry on.

6. Let it cook until *boom* — full emotional explosion.

Act surprised. Blame Mercury retrograde. Wonder why this keeps happening to you despite all those affirmations you chanted while brushing your teeth.

7. Survey the kitchen disaster.

Note the stains on your relationships, the burnt

bits of your mental and physical health, and the emotional goo splattered across your friendships and self-esteem.

8. Ask yourself the age-old question:

"Why didn't I just turn the heat down and release a little pressure?"

A tiny emotional exhale earlier could've saved the whole kitchen.

Recipe for a Healthy Human (Slow-Cooked Healing Edition)

Serves: Your future self and loved ones

Prep Time: However long you've avoided feeling your feelings

Cook Time: Ongoing, but totally worth it

Ingredients:

- 1 cup of honesty with yourself
- A handful of emotions you've been dodging
- A splash of courage
- Several deep breaths (freshly harvested)
- 1 supportive friend, therapist, or journal
- Optional: grace, patience, prayer, naps

Instructions:

1. Begin by opening the pressure cooker *before* turning the heat on.

This symbolizes emotional maturity and is highly recommended by nervous systems everywhere.

2. Gently toss in your feelings — yes, even the crunchy, awkward ones.

Don't rinse them. The rawness adds flavor.

3. Add a generous splash of honesty.

Stir well. This may cause temporary discomfort.

Perfectly normal.

4. Season with curiosity.

Ask yourself things like:

- "Why am I feeling this?"
- "What do I need right now?"
- "Am I spiraling or storytelling?"

  This step prevents overcooking.

5. Turn the heat to low.

Give your emotions TIME to soften.

(This is not an instant pot, this is a slow cooker.)

6. Add deep breaths, one at a time.

Repeat until the mixture stops bubbling aggressively.

7. Fold in support — a hug, a prayer, a grounding technique, a conversation, a walk.

This is the secret ingredient that changes the whole dish.

8. Taste and adjust.

Too spicy? Add calm.

Too salty? Add compassion.

Too bland? Add joy or rest.

9. Allow the mixture to simmer until your nervous system exclaims,

"Ahhhh, that's better."

10. Serve warm, with boundaries on the side. Pairs well with quiet confidence, aligned choices, and the ability to say "no."

And then there were the nights the humor couldn't reach. Anyway, onto the depressing poetic things I wrote in a state of heartbreak. Enjoy.

My heart is heavy with grief over loves that are no longer seen by my eyes but carried in my memories. The pain is proof that we loved. I will never get another night in my old home on the couch with snacks watching a show well past midnight. The keys belong to someone else and he broke mine. It's been years now but I can still feel what it was to be entwined with another soul through vows of forever. I will never get to travel through Europe enjoying pastries like I dreamt of with my love. Every one of my favorite songs reminds me of him, only he's no longer here to dance with me in the kitchen while we whisper promises of forever. The last words have been said, belongings were exchanged, even a last kiss was shared.

"We can't be together" sliced from my tongue a time or two, seemingly against my will. My heart begged me not to do it, not to walk away, but the circumstances made the choice for me.

What is one to do when we have to let go but we still love them? What are we supposed to do when the dreams we built and promises we made vanish with the person we used to share them with? What am I supposed to do when it's late and my heart calls for you but my head knows I can't pick up the phone?

Let go with love. That's the answer to all of those questions. Let go of what you hoped it would be with that person and the possibility of going back. Letting go completely is impossible since we're human. Letting go doesn't mean to forget them and the memories or even to stop loving. It means letting go of the future dreams you shared, acknowledging that you still want those things but also be open to different ways they may come to fruition. You loved that person yes, AND marriage, kids, travel, a house weren't reliant on that person. The pain shows us what we still want but we need to be open to different timelines and circumstances. Now to the second part: with love. Allow yourself to acknowledge why everything happened the way it did, accept it, but don't let it harden you. Sit in a cozy spot with your eyes closed. Allow the memories and positive feelings to flow through you. Picture that time your loved one held you as they said, "It's okay I'm right here and I'm not going anywhere". Allow the tears to rain down. Take your mind and heart back to the silly mishap that left you both laughing until you were in tears, feeling the closeness and pure joy. Allow that smile to crinkle your eyes and let the warmth of that memory visit you. When you're ready, take those feelings and memories and imagine that you're holding them in your hand. Close your hand, not too loose and not too tight, around the memories, love, feelings from this person and experience. Close your eyes and bring this gently closed fist of everything you shared with the being you're grieving to your heart. Imagine all of these beautiful things sinking into your heart and soul. They are safe, untouched, frozen in the past but accessible through your heart when you want to relive what was. Now picture yourself telling the other person anything that is on your heart. This could be reminiscing over the times you shared, questions about what they're up to now, updating them on your life, anything you didn't say in real life but wish you would have. Take this as an opportunity to give gratitude for all of the experiences, the beautiful and painful. The beautiful moments live in your heart as proof that love makes life brighter. The painful moments are opportunities to learn what we value and what our standards are as well as reminders of why it had to end. Bring to mind any dreams you envisioned with this person. I imagine you'll feel happy and excited revisiting them at first until the sadness hits. Smile at the beauty of this dream and offer up the sadness as a prayer, a hope that someday you and this person will be reunited in the place where there is no more pain or separation. This spark of light in my grief has given purpose to my pain and a connection to the people I have to love from afar.

Everyone we cross paths with leaves an imprint on us. Some offer kindness that softens us, others leave lessons that reshape us. Even the people who hurt me most taught me something about who I never want to become. Facing the darkness means acknowledging the pain they caused; sparking light begins with searching for even the smallest reason to forgive—not for them, but to free yourself.

Endings

There have been people in my life who met me in my darkness. Bound together by the darkness within both of us, they held me both in their arms and in the dark place we call unhealed wounds and unrealized potential. The darkness was a place of comfort for the both of us — not because it was safe, but because it was familiar.

Even relationship heartbreaks have served as catalysts in my life, particularly for my writing.

Here's a poem for the one I wanted to be the one:

To the One I Wanted to Be the One

I wanted you to be the one

Who brightened my life like the sun

After a cloudy day.

You were, for a time, I must say,

But quickly the sun faded into a cloud.

The whispers from God became so loud —

It's time to let him go,

For My plans, you do not know.

So I release you from my grip,

Out of my life you slip.

But I never forgot you.

A mind can block out, but the heart always remembers what made it turn blue.

I have to go now,

But I hope that somehow

I'll see you on the other side,

Where I can hold you and tell you how badly I wished I could've been your bride.

Grief never goes away or shrinks — new things just fill in around it.

Poetry on Grief

I.

Filled with sorrow

Over a love that was only mine to borrow.

Though I only had you for a time,

Parts of it were sublime,

For I am haunted by this love that was once mine.

But now there is nothing to have and to hold.

If love was enough I could have stayed,

But here I am, hurting from the mess that we made.

Everything tinged gray —

Together for never, but death won't do us part,

For we will be together again in the place we all start.

II.

When we were together we swore we'd never part,

But now here we are, worlds apart.

Stand by Me we used to sing,

And now here I am, selling my ring.

Stand by me,

Though forever we weren't meant to be.

Moonlight Serenade we both loved,

But the thought of you is now shoved to the back of my mind.

Around and around like a merry-go-round,

But now the quiet memories are the only sound —
Nights of laughter and dreams of happily ever after,
Dancing under lights, oh what a night.

III.

Creatures in Heaven still makes me think of you,

But it makes me so sad I don't know what to do.

I thought I knew you, but turns out I was wrong —

If only I didn't think of you every time I heard that song.

Forever in my heart, a scar that never fades,

But I have to remember: a spade is a spade.

Here I stand at the tombstones in the graveyard of my lost loves, writing letters and poems to those who can't see — for if they could see past themselves and into my soul, I wouldn't have had to lay them to rest in this place of old bones.

There We Were

There we were, my grief and me.

There we were, me and my grief.

Though our love was brief,

You sparked in me a belief

That I could love again,

Though I thought I couldn't back then.

Now there is nothing left to hold but my pen.

The proof of our love is etched into my heart,

Forever holding a part,

In the form of a scar.

No matter how far

We are in miles

Or in trials,

There you are

In every star

I wish upon.

I've waited so long

For you to change,

But for now it seems

I will only see you in my dreams,

Until we meet again

In the clouds.

Between now and then,

I want you to know I'm proud

Of how far you've come

And who you will become.

So long for now,

My love.

We experience grief because it's the price we pay for love, and it prepares us for what we're called for in heaven — a place of serenity and peace and no more loss. I hope to be reunited with everyone in Heaven, even those who hurt me deeply, because even they had an impact on me — even if it was just one positive memory or one valuable lesson. When I struggle to forgive, I remember the light in the darkness of the other person, if even just a spark.

Reflection Prompts

Who do I need to forgive?

Why are they the way they are? What traumas and darkness have they faced that influenced them?

What is something I ruminate on? How can I reframe the memory?

What parts of the memory can I allow myself to be sad about but also appreciate?

Chapter 11: Wings from Wounds

Although I felt unequipped and unprepared, I stepped up to the plate.

Motherhood didn't come with a manual, but it came with a mirror — one that reflected back all the parts of me that needed healing.

I quickly realized my son deserved better. He is and always has been, a spark of light in the darkness. He became the catalyst for a better life. I needed to break the cycle — to prioritize his safety, his happiness, his well-being... and to become a mother who had the light back in her eyes.

I didn't start a new life for myself.

At the time, I didn't love myself enough to know I

deserved better.

I did it for my son.

And somewhere in that process, Jesus led me to His Love and who He created me to be.

The life I built for him — one filled with peace, laughter, and light — ended up healing the parts of me that thought they'd never shine again.

I'm not saying you should have children to heal. But I am saying that my son became the *catalyst* that led me to my purpose.

If you ever find yourself faced with an impossible choice, I hope you choose the one that brings more light into the world.

Motherhood hasn't been the end of my life or my dreams.

It's been the *beginning*.

The catalyst for growth, healing, love, for writing this book, for starting my business, and for facing the shadows that used to scare me.

By worldly standards, motherhood is often painted as the end — the end of freedom, the end of youth, the end of ambition.

But what if it's *not* the end?

What if it's simply the end of life as you knew it — and the beginning of everything you were always meant to become?

Because when you hear that heartbeat for the first time, you realize: you'll never miss who you were before.

It changes everything — how you love, how you cherish life, how you see yourself.

Children are catalysts.

They reveal the darkness within us, not to shame us, but to show us the cracks where God can spark light.

Anyone who has ever hurt you is wounded themselves — and they were once a child, too.

If forgiveness feels impossible, don't force it.

But try, instead, to picture the person who hurt you as the child they once were.

What weight were they carrying?

Who failed to love or protect them?

Why are they acting out of pain instead of love?

You may not be able to fix them or stop the cycle, but you can meet that wounded version of them in your imagination — perhaps with your own inner child — and simply hold their hand. Maybe, together, you run through a field, both released from the chains that once held you down.

You can't erase the past, but you can meet the wounded where it all began and choose compassion over resentment.

You can forgive, not to excuse what happened, but to free yourself — and to stop the hurt from being passed forward.

We may not be able to give others the childhood they needed, but we can give *our own children* the one they deserve.

A childhood of safety and wonder — where they can run through fields making dandelion wishes, fall asleep mid-story, dance in the rain, and always know they are loved.

We can't change the past.

But we can shape the future within our own four walls. And that's how the cycle breaks — not in grand gestures, but in quiet, everyday love.

Motherhood became the mirror that showed me who I really was — and the map that guided me home.

Through the darkest valleys, I learned that light isn't something we find; it's something we *choose* to carry, if we allow the Light of the World to shine through us. My son was my catalyst, but the healing came from what I decided to do with that light.

Every lesson, every heartbreak, every prayer whispered in the dark led me here — to the framework that helped me rebuild my life piece by piece, from chaos to clarity. Not only was God there through everything, He was carrying me through, even when I didn't *feel* Him.

This next chapter isn't just about my story. It's about yours too — the one that's waiting to ignite.

Because we are all catalysts, meant to spark light from our own darkness.

Reflection Prompts

Who, or what, is a mirror for me?

What parts of the reflection am I happy with?

What parts of my reflection need healing?

What do those parts need to know? (Does 4 year old me need to know that she is safe and that adult you can take care of her? Does 13 year old me need to know that it's okay to not be perfect and that she is loved no matter what?)

Chapter 12: C.A.T.A.L.Y.S.T Framework

You may notice that I don't go into every dark detail of my story. That's intentional. This book isn't about comparing my pain to yours or trying to prove who suffered more. I want this to be a space where you can bring your own story, your own darkness, and use it as a catalyst for light. My framework isn't a prescription — it's a guide. How you apply it will look different than how I did, and that's exactly the point. The power comes from making it your own.

Before I share this framework, I want to be honest with you. This isn't a checklist. It's not eight steps you complete and graduate from. Healing isn't linear, and neither is this. You may move through these in order, or you may find yourself circling back to C when you thought you were on T. That's not failure — that's being human. The Holy Spirit doesn't work on our timeline. He works on His.

This framework is a guide, not a gospel. The Gospel is the Gospel. This is just one woman's map of how she let Jesus walk her out of the dark. How you apply it will look different than how I did, and that's exactly the point. The power comes from making it your own.

The Catalyst Framework: A Faith-Rooted Path Darkness to Light

C — Cry & Connect

"Jesus wept." — John 11:35

The shortest verse in the Bible is also one of the most freeing. Jesus cried. Standing at the tomb of His friend Lazarus — knowing full well He was about to raise him from the dead — He still wept.

He didn't skip the grief because He knew the outcome. He honored it.

Crying isn't weakness. Tears are how the body releases what words cannot. Modern research backs what scripture already showed us: emotional tears actually contain stress hormones the body needs to expel. God designed us to cry.

What this looks like in practice:

- Letting yourself feel the wave when it comes, instead of swallowing it down

- Naming the emotion out loud (anger, grief, betrayal, fear) — vague feelings have power; named ones become workable
- Reaching for one safe person — a sister, a friend, a mentor — and saying "I'm not okay"
- Bringing your tears to Jesus directly, not cleaned up first

The trap to watch for:

We are often taught to "offer it up" before we've actually felt it. Offering up a wound you haven't acknowledged isn't redemptive suffering — it's spiritual bypassing. You cannot offer to God what you refuse to look at. Feel it first. Then offer.

A small practice:

When tears come, set a timer for ten minutes. Don't perform, don't analyze, don't fix. Just cry. When the timer ends, place your hand on your heart and say: "Jesus, you saw that. Thank you for not leaving."

A — Acknowledge & Allow

"He heals the brokenhearted and binds up their wounds." — Psalm 147:3

Acknowledgment is the act of saying: this happened, and it hurt. No qualifying it. No comparing it to someone whose story sounds worse. No rushing to "but God is good" before you've sat with "but this was not."

Allowing is the next layer: letting the emotion exist in your body without judging yourself for having it. Anger is information. Sadness is sacred. Even bitterness, when acknowledged, can become a doorway — but only if you stop pretending it's not there.

The trap to watch for:

Spiritual bypassing wears a holy mask. It sounds like "I should be over this by now," or "A real Christian women would forgive faster," or "I'm being ungrateful." These are not the voice of the Holy Spirit. The Holy Spirit convicts; He does not shame. If a thought leaves you feeling small, hidden, or unworthy of being held — that's not Him.

What allowing does NOT mean:

- It doesn't mean acting on every emotion
- It doesn't mean staying in unsafe situations
- It doesn't mean abandoning forgiveness as a destination

What it does mean:

- You stop fighting yourself.
- You let the wave move through.
- Resistance is what keeps us stuck.
- Acknowledgment is what unsticks us.

A small practice:

Finish this sentence on paper, no censor: "I am allowed to feel ___ about ___ because ___." Read it back. Notice if your inner critic shows up. Tell her gently: "Not today. Today I'm just allowing."

T — Therapy & Tools

"Plans fail for lack of counsel, but with many advisers they succeed." — Proverbs 15:22

You are not meant to heal alone. Even Jesus had the Twelve. Even Mary had Elizabeth. Isolation is where wounds fester; community and equipped guides are where they mend.

A good therapist is not a replacement for prayer — she is an answer to it. God uses trained hands. He used a doctor named Luke to write a Gospel. He uses trained counselors today. Find one who respects your faith, ideally one who shares it.

Tools that have helped me, and that women I love have leaned on:

- Therapy — especially trauma-informed modalities like EMDR, somatic therapy, or Internal Family Systems for those carrying childhood wounds
- Spiritual direction — different from therapy; a trained companion (often through your parish or diocese) who walks with you in prayer
- The Sacrament of Reconciliation / Confession — for Catholic women, the ongoing grace of being heard by Christ through His priest is its own healing

- Adoration — sitting in silence before the Eucharist when words won't come
- Journaling — especially "letter writing" to the people you can't or shouldn't speak to
- Somatic practices — gentle yoga, walking, breathwork; trauma lives in the body and the body has to be part of the healing
- Books — The Body Keeps the Score by Bessel van der Kolk for the science; Searching for and Maintaining Peace by Jacques Philippe for the spiritual companion
- Prayer routines — a daily Rosary, lectio divina for just five minutes with scripture

and coffee, or an open conversation with Jesus about what is on your heart.

The trap to watch for:

Believing that needing professional help means your faith is weak. It doesn't. A broken arm needs a doctor and prayer. So does a broken heart. God works through both.

A permission slip:

You are allowed to take medication if you need it. You are allowed to see a therapist weekly. You are allowed to need help. None of this disqualifies you from holiness.

A — Articulate & Share

"They overcame him by the blood of the Lamb and by the word of their testimony." — Revelation 12:11

There is power in telling your story. Scripture says so. Your testimony — the unfiltered truth of what you survived and how God met you in it — is part of how the kingdom comes.

But "share" doesn't mean "broadcast." Articulation is about finding your words for your own experience, then choosing — wisely, prayerfully — who gets to hear them.

Three layers of sharing, from inside out:

1. With yourself (journaling, voice memos, letters never sent). This is where the real articulation begins. You cannot share with others what you have not first put words to inside yourself. Write the unedited version. Burn it if you need to. The point is naming.

2. With a trusted few. A small circle — your sister, your spiritual director, a close friend, your therapist. People who have earned the right to hear your story by their consistency and their care. Not everyone has earned that right, and it is not unloving to keep your story from people who haven't.

3. With the world (when called). This is the testimony stage — and it's not for everyone, and it's not always. Some stories are meant to be told only to one trusted person. Some are meant for a memoir. Some are meant only for God. Discernment matters. Pray about it.

The trap to watch for:

Either silencing yourself entirely ("nobody wants to hear it / it'll burden them / I should just pray about it") or oversharing to the wrong audiences (social media, casual acquaintances, anyone who will listen). Both are forms of mismanaging the gift of your story.

A guiding question:

Will telling this story to this person, in this moment, bring more light into the world — or am I bleeding on people who didn't cut me?

L—La Vie en Rose

"Finally, brothers, whatever is true, whatever is honorable, whatever is just, whatever is pure, whatever is lovely, whatever is commendable, if

there is any excellence, if there is anything worthy of praise, think about these things." — Philippians 4:8

This is not toxic positivity. This is the disciplined practice of looking for the hidden gift inside the hardest things — after you have grieved, not instead of grieving.

Romans 8:28 says God works all things for the good of those who love Him. Not that all things are good. But that all things — even the unspeakable ones — can be woven by Him into something redemptive. That's the rose-colored lens. Not pretending the thorns don't exist, but trusting the bloom is coming.

What La Vie en Rose looks like in practice:

- Asking, after a season of grief: "What did this teach me that I couldn't have learned any other way?"
- Naming three small lights from the darkest day (a song that found you, a stranger's kindness, a verse that landed)
- Reframing without minimizing: "I lost so much, AND I gained a sensitivity to others' pain I didn't have before"
- Looking at your younger self with the tenderness you'd give your own daughter

The trap to watch for:

Skipping straight to this step. Trying to find the "lesson" before you've felt the loss. The rose-colored glasses don't work if you put them on while you're still bleeding — you just blur the wound. Grieve first. Reframe after. Both are holy.

A small practice:

At the end of a hard week, write three columns: What hurt this week. What I learned. Where I saw God anyway. Don't force the second two columns. Let them come slowly, over time.

Y — Yield to Purpose

"For I know the plans I have for you, declares the Lord, plans for welfare and not for evil, to give you a future and a hope." — Jeremiah 29:11

Yielding is the act of saying Thy will be done — and meaning it. Not as defeat, but as trust. It's Mary's fiat — "let it be done unto me according to thy word." It's the moment in the garden when Jesus prayed not my will, but Yours.

This is the hardest letter. Surrender goes against every survival instinct trauma installed in us. We were hurt because we had no control, so we learned to grasp for it. Yielding feels like becoming the helpless little girl again. But there's a profound difference: now we yield to a Father who is good, who never leaves, and who is writing a story we cannot yet see.

Yielding is not:

- Passivity (you still act; you still set boundaries; you still leave unsafe places)
- Pretending you understand (you often won't; that's the point)

- Being a doormat (Jesus surrendered to the Father, never to abusers)

Yielding IS:

- Releasing your timeline
- Trusting that even what feels like a delay is direction
- Believing your pain is not wasted in His economy
- Letting God write the next chapter, even if you don't get to read ahead

The trap to watch for:

Confusing yielding with self-abandonment. Some of us — especially those wounded in childhood — were taught that being good meant disappearing. Yielding to God is not disappearing. He yields toward you, not against you. He wants the real you to emerge, not the suppressed, smaller version that learned to survive.

A prayer:

Jesus, I don't understand. I don't see the plan. I'm scared of what surrender will cost me. But I trust You more than I trust my own grip. Take it. All of it. I'll keep showing up.

S — See Others

"Carry each other's burdens, and in this way you will fulfill the law of Christ." — Galatians 6:2

Pain has a way of turning us inward. That's natural — a wound demands attention. But there is a moment in healing where the kindest thing you can do for yourself is gently turn outward.

Not as escapism. Not as performance. But because we are made for communion, and because seeing another person's pain is one of the most healing acts there is — for them and for you.

The two directions of "See Others":

1. Seeing those still in the dark. When you've walked through something and come out, you carry a lamp. Other women — many of them silent, ashamed, alone — are still in the tunnel you just exited. Your simple presence, your quiet "me too," your mentorship or friendship, can be the spark they need. This is part of why I wrote this book.

2. Seeing those who hurt you. This is harder. It doesn't mean reconciling, and it never means

returning to harm. But it does mean — when you're ready — looking at the people who wounded you and seeing the wounded children they once were. Hurt people hurt people. Recognizing this doesn't excuse what they did. It frees you from carrying their weight.

The trap to watch for:

Skipping straight to "seeing others" as a way to avoid your own healing. Service from an unhealed place is performance. Service from a healed place — even partially healed — is ministry. Make sure you're not bandaging others to avoid looking at your own wounds.

A small practice:

Once a week, do one act of seeing — a text to a friend you sense is struggling, a meal for a new mom, a real conversation with the cashier. Not big. Just real.

T — Transform & Trust

"And we know that for those who love God all things work together for good, for those who are called according to His purpose." — Romans 8:28

This is the culmination — and also the recommitment. Transformation is the fruit of all the previous letters. Trust is the soil they grow in.

Transformation doesn't mean you become unrecognizable. It means the wounded version of you becomes the witnessing version — the one who can say to another woman in the dark, "I've been there. Light is real. Let me show you."

Trust isn't a feeling. It's a daily decision. Some mornings you'll wake up and trust will feel easy. Other mornings, the old fears will roar back, and you'll have to whisper "I trust You, Jesus" through gritted teeth. Both count. Both are faith.

Signs you are transforming (even when it doesn't feel like it):

- Your triggers don't level you the way they used to
- You can tell your story without falling apart
- You recognize patterns earlier — and choose differently

- You catch yourself comforting your inner child instead of shaming her
- You laugh more freely, and cry more honestly
- The people in your life are becoming healthier — because you are

The trap to watch for:

Believing transformation has to be dramatic to count. Most transformation is quiet. It's the tenth time you choose peace over revenge. The hundredth time you go to Mass when you don't feel like it. The morning you realize you haven't checked his social media in a month. Small, faithful, ordinary. That's how saints are made.

The closing truth:

You will not finish this framework. Not in this life. There will always be a new layer to grieve, a new letter to revisit, a new way Jesus wants to meet you. That's not failure — that's the journey of becoming. Heaven is where the framework ends. Until then, we walk it together.

A Final Word on Walking the Framework

The eight letters are not a staircase. They are a spiral. You will revisit C when you thought you were on T. You will need to allow again what you thought you had allowed. New griefs will surface old ones. This is normal.

What matters is not where you are on the framework. What matters is that you keep walking — and that you let Jesus walk it with you.

You are not behind. You are not failing. You are becoming.

"He who began a good work in you will bring it to completion at the day of Jesus Christ." — Philippians 1:6

Reflection Prompts for the Framework

Which letter feels easiest for you right now? Why?

Which letter feels hardest? What might that be telling you?

Where do you tend to skip ahead? Where do you tend to get stuck?

Who in your life models one of these letters well?

What can you learn from her?

Where is Jesus already meeting you in this framework, even if you didn't have words for it before?

Chapter 13: Be the Light

I share my story not only to connect with my readers, let others know they are not alone in their sufferings, but to spread this message: the darkness will make you appreciate the light more and every light was sparked in darkness. Whoever you are, wherever you are, I want you to know that no matter what you are facing or have faced, no matter how impossible it may seem, how painful it is, there is always light that can be sparked in the darkness. Allow yourself to acknowledge the darkness and face the shadows but don't dwell for too long before you use the darkness to catalyze you into the light.

Sharing your story is a service to yourself and to others.

This is not a book about system reform, it's a book about healing things within us. The system will always be broken or if it's "fixed" it often hurts someone else. It's not even about preventing things like marrying the wrong one, it's about allowing Jesus to spark light in the darkness of those experiences. God can change the world one spark at a time, all we need to do is cooperate and surrender to Him.

Finding My Light » Catalyst Spark

When I look in the mirror today, I still see the dark circles—but I also see the spark. And I wouldn't trade it for anything. As long as I'm here on earth I will face darkness and now I know that life isn't about avoiding the darkness because some things are inevitable. It's about sparking light and using the darkness as a catalyst for good things, like helping others or new beginnings.

This isn't just my story. It's a framework for transformation. Because pain, when processed with intention, becomes purpose. And purpose, when shared, becomes impact."

Closing Reflection

For years, I searched for light outside myself and outside of God — in people, in places, in plans that kept falling apart.

But the truth is, light was never lost. It was only waiting.

My son's laughter reminded me that love can exist without fear.

Faith reminded me that joy is always born from surrender.

And healing reminded me that even in ashes, there's always something ready to bloom.

Because sometimes, the greatest spark doesn't come from escaping the fire — but from learning how to rise from it. The difference between those who find the sparks of light and those who stay in the darkness of the ashes is their willingness to reach for the hand who so lovingly wants to hold ours.

We're all blessed with a spark.

Life will dim it.

It faintly returns.

The fire of the suffering burns everything to the ground.

But we can find light through the ashes.

We must feel the grief of the burning first.

Then we can take our spark

Light a torch with it

Pass it forward

Use the darkness and the light as a catalyst

To become the light.

So, will you choose the sparks of light?

All it takes is one spark of love, light,

laughter.

Together,

We can light the world on fire.

The moments that almost broke me didn't end my story—they became the reason I now get to help others rewrite theirs.

What once felt like pain now carries purpose. And what once felt like an ending became the beginning of everything.

And maybe that's the point—

that the hardest parts of our lives aren't meant to

stop us, but to shape us into who we were always meant to become.

Final Reflection Prompts

How can I use my suffering for good?

What did I need to hear when I was going through my darkest times?

How can I serve someone else?

Epilogue

We can't recognize light without first knowing darkness.

My mission now is to spark more light in the world by creating a positive news platform—somewhere people can go to remember that good still exists. I would love to hear *your* story and the sparks of light in your life. Maybe it's a promotion, a breathtaking sunset, a new friendship, an engagement, a book that moved you—anything that lifted your spirit. I'd be honored to hear it and share it on my podcast. Send your sparks to brooke@smcllc.co.

Writing this book brought up memories I had long tucked away—memories that once felt too heavy to hold. But facing them again reminded me that pain often carries purpose. In releasing these stories, I experienced something deeply healing, something I didn't expect.

It came to me in a dream—one that, in the past, would have been a full-blown nightmare. I dreamt I was taken from my family again, but this time I was an adult. Instead of the terror and panic I once felt as a child, I chose to look through rose-colored glasses. I searched for the moment of meaning, the spark that would one day inspire me to write this book and help someone else. And when I allowed myself to see life *la vie en rose*, the fear softened. I wasn't afraid anymore.

About the Author

Brooke is a storyteller, mother, creator, and founder of LifeStories Heirlooms, an heirloom-centered brand dedicated to preserving the moments, memories, and meaning that shape who we are.

After walking through childhood trauma, heartbreak, mental health battles, and profound healing, she discovered that her purpose was not found in escaping her darkness — but in transforming it.

Her mission is to spark more light in the world by helping others find beauty, purpose, and hope within their own stories.

She lives with her son, her biggest inspiration and brightest light.

www.ingramcontent.com/pod-product-compliance
Lightning Source LLC
LaVergne TN
LVHW041707070526
838199LV00045B/1242